MAINE LAW DOCUMENTS FOR THE PEOPLE;

CONTAINING

THE MAINE LIQUOR LAW,

HON. NEAL DOW AND PROF. STEWART ON THE WORKINGS OF THE LAW—LETTER OF NEAL DOW IN REPLY TO O. LUND'S, ON THE PRESENT INFLUENCE OF THE LAW—CONSTITUTIONAL QUESTION—PROHIBITORY UNITED STATES LAW AMONG THE INDIAN TRIBES—TWENTY-THREE OBJECTIONS TO THE LAW CONSIDERED AND ANSWERED—ECONOMY OF THE MAINE LIQUOR LAW—PROHIBITORY LAW—LOOK AT YOUR TAXES—ALBERT BARNES ON THE MAINE LAW—SHALL WE HAVE THE MAINE LAW?—NATIONAL LEGISLATON, ETC.

Compiled by ORLANDO LUND,

Author of "Temperance Man's Declaration of Rights"—"Downfall of the Tyrant"—"Order of the Sons of Temperance, its Origin, History," &c., &c.

HOMER, N. Y.:

L. BALDWIN, JR., PRINTER, ELMIRA, N. Y.

1853.

The object of the compiler in throwing together the Papers and Documents herein containd in the present form, is to place within the reach of all, not only the law itself, but facts, statements and arguments, showing its practical influence wherever introduced and properly sustained; together with the reasons and constitutionality of such prohibitory Law.

The papers selected are from our best writers, and all bear directly on the great question now at issue before the people.

Anecdote and story have in a great measure lost their power What the people want at the present time, are facts, and a thorough, practical, temperance sentiment, embodied in law, based on great, moral principles.

Friends of Temperance—friends of Humanity—friends of your country—friends of your God—*such practical sentiment* you find in the following pages. Read, and circulate with a liberal hand.

O. LUND.

THE MAINE LIQUOR LAW.

An Act for the Suppression of Drinking-Houses and Tippling-Shops.

Be it enacted by the Senate and House of Representatives in Legislature assembled, as follows:

SECTION 1. No person shall be allowed at any time to manufacture or sell, by himself, his clerk, servant or agent, directly or indirectly, any spirituous or intoxicating liquors, or any mixed liquors, a part of which is spirituous or intoxicating, except as hereafter provided.

SEC. 2. The selectmen of any town, and mayor and aldermen of any city, on the first Monday of May annually, or as soon thereafter as may be convenient, may appoint some suitable person as the agent of said town or city, to sell at some central or convenient place within said town or city, spirits, wines, or other intoxicating liquors, to be used for medicinal and mechanical purposes and no other: and said agent shall receive such compensation for his services as the board appointing him shall prescribe; and shall in the sale of such liquors, conform to such rules and regulations as the selectmen or mayor and aldermen as aforesaid, shall prescribe for that purpose. And such agent, appointed as aforesaid, shall hold his situation for one year, unless sooner removed by the board from which he received his appointment, as he may be at any time, at the pleasure of said board.

SEC. 3. Such agent shall receive a certificate from the mayor and aldermen or selectmen by whom he has been appointed, authorizing him as the agent of such town or city, to sell intoxicating liquors for medicinal and mechanical purposes only; but such certificate shall not be delivered to the person so appointed, until he shall have executed and delivered to said board a bond, with two good and sufficient sureties, in the sum of six hundred dollars, in substance as follows:

Know all men, that we, ——— as principal, and ——— as sureties, are holden and stand firmly bound to the inhabitants of the town of ———, (or city, as the case may be,) in the sum of six hundred dollars, to be paid them, to which payment we bind ourselves, our heirs, executors, and administrators, firmly by these presents. Sealed with our seals, and dated this —— day of —— A. D. ——

The condition of this obligation is such, that whereas the above bounden ——— has been duly appointed an agent for the town (or city) of ——— to sell, within, and for and on account of said town (or city) intoxicating liquors for medicinal and mechanical purposes and no other, until the —— day of —— A. D. ——, unless sooner removed from said agency.

Now if the said ——— shall in all respects conform to the provisions of the law relating to the business for which he is appointed, and to such rules and regulations as now are or shall be from time to time established by the board making the appointment, then this obligation to be void; otherwise to remain in full force.

Sec. 4. If any person, by himself, clerk, servant or agent, shall at any time sell any spirituous or intoxicating liquors, or any mixed liquors, part of which is intoxicating, in violation of the provisions of this act, he shall forfeit and pay on the first conviction, ten dollars and the costs of prosecution, and shall stand committed until the same be paid; on the second conviction he shall pay twenty dollars and the costs of prosecution, and shall stand committed until the same be paid; on the third and every subsequent conviction, he shall pay twenty dollars and the costs of prosecution, and shall be imprisoned in the common jail, not less than three months, nor more than six months, and in default of the payment of the fines and costs prescribed by this section for the first and second convictions, the convict shall not be entitled to the benefit of chapter 175 of the revised statutes, until he shall have been imprisoned two months; and in default of payment of fines and costs provided for the third and every subsequent conviction, he shall not be entitled to the benefit of said chapter 175 of the revised statutes until he shall have been imprisoned four months. And if any clerk, servant, agent or other person in the employment or on the premises of another, shall violate the provisions of this section, he shall be held equally guilty with the principal, and on conviction shall suffer the same penalty.

Sec. 5. Any forfeiture or penalty arising under the above section, may be recovered by an action of debt, or by complaint before any justice of the peace, or judge of any municipal or police court, in the county where the offence was committed. And the forfeiture so recovered shall go to the town where the convicted party resides, for the use of the poor; and the prosecutor or complainant may be admitted as a witness in the trial. And if any one of the selectmen or board of mayor and aldermen shall approve of the commencement of any such suit, by endorsing his name upon the writ, the defendant shall in no event recover any costs; and in all actions of debt arising under this section the fines and forfeitures suffered by the defendant, shall be the same as if the action had been by complaint. And it shall be the duty of the mayor and aldermen of any city, and selectmen of any town, to commence an action in behalf of said town or city, against any person guilty of a violation of any of the provisions of this act, on being informed of the same, and being furnished with proof of the fact.

SEC. 6. If any person shall claim an appeal from a judgment rendered against him by any judge or justice, on the trial of such action or complaint, he shall before the appeal shall be allowed, recognize in the sum of one hundred dollars, with two good and sufficient sureties, in every case so appealed, to prosecute his appeal, and to pay all costs, fines and penalties that may be awarded against him, upon a final disposition of such suit or complaint. And before his appeal shall be allowed, he shall also in every case, give a bond with two other good and sufficient sureties, running to the town or city where the offence was committed, in the sum of two hundred dollars, that he will not, during the pendency of such appeal, violate any of the provisions of this act. And no recognizance or bond shall be taken in cases arising under this act, except by the justice or judge before whom the trial was had; and the defendant shall be held to advance the jury fees in every case of appeal in action of debt; and in the event of a final conviction before a jury, the defendant shall pay and suffer double the amount of fines penalties and imprisonment awarded against him by the justice or judge from whose judgement the appeal was made. The forfeiture for all bonds and recognizances given in pursuance of this act, shall go to the town or city where the offence was committed, for the use of the poor; and if the recognizances and bonds mentioned in this section shall not be given within twenty-four hours after the judgment, the appeal shall not be allowed; the defendant in the meantime to stand committed.

SEC. 7. The mayor and aldermen of any city, and the selectmen of any town, whenever complaint shall be made to them that a breach of the conditions of the bond given by any person appointed under this act, has been committed, shall notify the person complained of, and if upon a hearing of the parties it shall appear that any breach has been committed, they shall revoke and make void his appointment. And whenever a breach of any bond given to the inhabitants of any city or town in pursuance of any of the provisions of this act, shall be made known to the mayor and aldermen, or selectman, or shall in any manner come to their knowledge, they or some of them shall, at the expense and for the use of such city or town, cause the bond to be put in suit in any court proper to try the same.

SEC. 8. No person shall be allowed to be a manufacturer of any spirituous or intoxicating liquor, or common seller thereof without being duly appointed as aforesaid, on pain of forfeiting on the first conviction, the sum of one hundred dollars and costs of prosecution, and in default of the payment thereof, the person so convicted shall be imprisoned sixty days in the common jail; and on the second conviction, the person so convicted shall pay the sum of two hundred dollars and costs of prosecution, and in default of payment, shall be imprisoned four months in the common jail; and on the third and every subsequent conviction, shall pay the sum of two hundred dollars, and shall be imprisoned four months in the common jail of the county where the offence was committed; said penalties to be recovered before any court of competent jurisdiction, by indictment, or by action of debt in the name of the city or town where the offence shall be committed. And whenever a default shall be had of any recognizances arising under this act, "scire facias" shall be issued, returnable at the next term, and the same shall not be continued, unless for good cause, satisfactory to the court.

Sec. 9. No person engaged in the unlawful traffic in intoxicating liquors shall be competent to sit upon any jury in any case arising from this act, and when information shall be communicated to the court, that any member of any panel is engaged in such traffic, or that he is believed to be so engaged, the court shall inquire of the juryman of whom such belief is entertained; and no answer which he shall make shall be used against him in any case arising under this act; but if he shall answer falsely, he shall be incapable of serving on any jury in this state; but he may decline to answer, in which case he shall be discharged by the court from all further attendance as a juryman.

Sec. 10. All cases arising under this act, whether by action, indictment or complaint, which shall come before a superior court, either by appeal or original entry, shall take precedence in said court of all other business, except those criminal cases in which the parties are actually under arrest awaiting a trial; and the court and the prosecuting officer shall not have authority to enter a nolle prosequi, or to grant a continuance in any case arising under this act, either before or after the verdict, except where the purposes of justice shall require it.

Sec. 11. If any three persons, voters in the town or city where the complaint shall be made, shall, before any justice of the peace or judge of municipal or police court, make complaint under oath or affirmation, that they have reason to believe, and do believe that spirituous or intoxicating liquors are kept or deposited, and intended for sale, by any person not authorized to sell the same in said city or town under the provisions of this act, in any store, shop, warehouse or other building or place in said city or town, said justice or judge shall issue his warrant of search to any sheriff, city marshall or deputy, or to any constable, who shall proceed to search the premises described in said warrant, and if any spirituous or intoxicating liquors are found therein, he shall seize the same, and convey them to some place of security, where he shall keep them until final action is had thereon. But no dwelling-house, in which or in part of which, a shop is not kept, shall be searched, unless at least one of said complainants shall testify to some acts of sale of intoxicating liquors therein, by the occupant thereof, or by his consent or permission, within at least one month of the time of making said complaint. And the owner or keeper of such liquors, seized as aforesaid, if he shall be known to the officer seizing the same, shall be summoned forthwith before the justice or judge by whose warrant the liquors were seized, and if he fails to appear, or unless he can show by positive proof, that said liquors are of foreign production, that they have been imported under the laws of the United States, and in accordance therewith—that they are contained in the original packages in which the were imported and in quantities not less than the laws of the United States prescribe, they shall be declared forfeited, and shall be destroyed by authority of the written order to that effect, of said justice or judge, and in his presence, or in the presence of some person appointed by him, to witness the destruction thereof, and who shall join with the officer by whom they shall have been destroyed, in attesting that fact upon the back of the order by authority of which it was done; and the owner or keeper of such liquors shall pay a fine of twenty dollars and costs, or stand committed for thirty days, in default of payment, if in the opinion of the court, said liquors shall have been kept or deposited for the purposes of sale. And if the owner or possessor of any liquors seized in pursuance of this section, shall set up the claim that they heve been regularly imported under the laws of the United States, and that they are contained in the original packages, the custom-house certificates of importation and proofs of marks on the casks or packages corresponding hereto,shall not be received as evidence that the liquors contained in said packages are those actually imported therein.

SEC. 12. If the owner, keeper or possessor of liquors, seized under the provisions of this act, shall be unknown to the officer seizing the same they shall not be condemned until they shall have been advertised, with the number and description of the packages as near as may be, for two weeks, by posting up a written description of the same in some public place; that if such liquors are actually the property of any city or town in the state, and were so at the time of the seizure, purchased for sale by the agent of said city or town, for medicinal or mechanical purposes only, in pursuance of the provisions of this act, they may not be destroyed; but upon satisfactory proof of such ownership, within said two weeks, before the justice or judge by whose authority said liquors were seized, said justice or judge shall deliver to the agent of said city or town an order to the officer having said liquors in custody, whereupon said officer shall deliver them to said agent, taking his receipt therefor on the back of said order, which shall be returned to said justice or judge.

SEC. 13. If any person claiming any liquors seized as aforesaid, shal appeal from the judgment of any justice or judge, by whose authority the seizure was made, to the district court, before his appeal shall be allowed, he shall give a bond in the sum of two hundred dollars, with two good and sufficient sureties, to prosecute his appeal and to pay all fines and costs which may be awarded against him; and in the case of any such appeal, where the qcantity of liquor so seized shall exceed five gallons, if the final decision shall be against the appellant, that suchliquors were intended by him for sale, he shall be adjudged by the court a common seller of intoxicating liquors, and shall be subject to the penalties ·vided for in section eight of this act; and said liquors shall be destroyed as provided for in section eleven. But nothing contained in this act shall be construed to prevent any chemist, artist or manufacturer, in whose art or trade they may be necessary, from keeping at his place of business such reasonable and proper quantity of distilled liquors as he may have occasion to use in his art or trade, but not for sale.

SEC. 14. It shall be the duty of any mayor, alderman, selectman assessor, city marshall or deputy or constable, if he shall have information that any intoxicating liquors are kept or sold in any tent, shanty, hut or place of any kind for selling refreshments in any public place, on or near the ground of any cattle show, agricultural exhibition, military muster, or public occasion of any kind, to search such suspected place, and if such officer shall find upon the premises any intoxicating drinks, he shall seize them, and arrest the keeper or keepers of such place, and take them forthwith, or as soon as may be, before some justice or judge of a municipal or police court, with the liquors so found and seized, and upon proof that said liquors are intoxicating, that they were found in possession of the accused, in a tent, shanty or other place as aforesaid, he or they shall be sentenced to imprisonment in the county jail for thirty days, and the liquor so seized shall be destroyed by order of said justice or judge.

SEC. 15. If any person arrested under the preceeding section, and sentenced as aforesaid, shall claim an appeal, before his appeal shall be allowed, he shall give a bond in the sum of one hundred dollars, with two good and sufficient sureties, that he will prosecute his appeal, and pay all fines, costs andpenalties which may be awarded against him.—And if on such appeal, the verdict of the jury be against him, he shall in addition to the penalty awarded by the lower court, pay a fine of twenty dollars. In all cases of appeal arising under this act, from the judgment of a justice or judge of any municipal or police court to the district court, except where the proceeding is by action of debt, they shall be conducted in said district court by the prosecuting officer of the government—and said officer shall be entitled to receive all costs taxable to the state, in all criminul proceedings under this act, in addition to the salary allowed to such officer by law—but no costs in such cases shall be remitted by the prosecuting officer or the court. In any suit, complaint, indictment or other proceeding against any person for a violation of any of the provisions of this act, other than for the first offence, it shall not be requisite to set forth particularly the record of a former conviction, but it shall be sufficient to alledge briefly that such person has been convicted of a violation of the fourth section of this act, or as a common seller, as the case may be, and such allegation in any civil or criminal process in any stage of the procedings, before final judgment may be amended without terms and as a matter of right.

SEC. 16. All payments or compensations for liquor sold in violation of law, whether in money, labor or other property, either real or personal, shall be held and considered to have been received in violation of la and without consideration, and against law, equity and good conscience and all sales, transfers and conveyances, mortgages, liens, attachments, pledges and securities of every kind, which either in whole or in part shall have been for or on account of spirituous or intoxicating liquors, shall be utterly null and void against all persons and in all cases, and no rights of any kind shall be acquired thereby; and in any action either at law or equity, touching such real or personal estate, the purchaser of such liquors may be a witness for either party. And no action of any kind shall be maintained in any court in this state, either in whole or in part, for intoxicating or spirituous liquors sold in any other state or county whatever, nor shall any action of any kind be had or maintained in any court in this state, for the recovery or possession of intoxicating or spirituous liquors or the value thereof.

SEC. 17. All the provisions of this act relating to towns shall be applicable to cities and plantations; and those relating to selectmen shall also be applied to the mayor and aldermen of cities and assessors of plantations.

SEC. 18. The act entitled "An Act to restrict the sale of intoxicating drinks," approved August sixth, one thousand eight hundred and forty-six, is hereby repealed, except the thirteen sections, from section ten to section twenty-two inclusive, saving or reserving all actions or other prceedings, which are already commenced by authority of the same; and all other acts or parts of acts inconsistent with this act, are hereby repealed. This act to take effect from and after its approval by the governor.

(Approved June 2, 1851.)

The Working of the Law.

FROM THE QUARTERLY REPORT OF THE MAYOR OF PORTLAND.

MAYOR'S OFFICE, SEPT., 1851.

TO THE CITIZENS OF PORTLAND:

The "Act for the Suppression of Drinking-Houses and Tippling-Shops," passed at the last session of the Legislature, has been in operation in this city for about three months, and I think it proper to give the people of Portland some definite information of its results.

At the time of its passage there was supposed to be in this city from 200 to 300 shops and other places where intoxicating liquors were sold to all comers. At the present time there are no places where such liquors are sold openly, and only a few where they are sold at all, and that with great caution and secresy, and only to those who are personally known to the keepers, and who can be relied upon not to betray them to the authorities. These places, with one, (pcssibly with two) exceptions, are of the lowest character; and so far as they sell these liquors at all, minister to the depraved appetites of the basest part of our population; *but the* keepers of these places will soon be brought to justice, *so that the traffic in* intoxicating liquors, to be used as a drink, will be *entirely extinguished* in this city. The shops which I allude to are kept *almost exclusively* by foreigners, and the few persons who are now brought to the lock-up in the watch house, are the customers of these places, and are themselves foreigners almost without exception. The stock of liquors which the keepers of these places had on hand when the law went into operation will soon be exhausted, and some difficulty will be found by them in replenishing their stores, as the law will enable us to stop entirely the supplies of these liquors, which have hitherto been received by railroad principallyandsteamboat.

All these persons who are now selling these liquors unlawfully in Portland are doing it on a very small scale. The supplies which the most of them keep on hand are extremely limited in amount, and every precaution is used to conceal them from the police. In one shop searched was found less than one quart in two small bottles; in another were found only three bottles, containing less than three quarts, concealed in a cellar, behind a board; in another, the liquor was found under the floor, buried in the earth—and some has been found in deeper concealment.

Three months ago there were in this city several wholesale dealers in liqnors; but at the present time there is not one—the wholesale business ceased entirely, when the law went into operation. There was but one distillery in the State, at the time of the enactment of this law although another was in progress on a very large scale. Operations on the latter were promptly stopped, and the other has been demolished. At the present time there is no distillery in this State.

* * * * * *

The operation of the law in this city has effected a marked change for the better, in every department which is under the care of the police. The night police has comparatively little or nothing to do; there are few or no street brawls, and it is very seldom that the police or watch are called upon to interfere in any quarrels or disturbances of any kind in shops or houses in any part of the city. Before the enactment of this law, scarcely a night passed over without some disturbance of this description, and sometimes the police were called upon to quell many such disturbances in a single night.

At the commencement of the present year, scarcely a night passed over without the committal to the watch-house of more or less intemperate persons, and sometimes many such were committed in a single night. The practice formerly was to commit no intoxicated persons who were quiet and able to get home. At present, the orders to the police and watch are to arrest all persons found in the streets or other public places, either by night or by day, who exhibit unmistakable signs of intoxication; yet with all this rigor the arrests for this cause are very few—sometimes a week or more, and once a fortnight having elapsed without any committal; and were it not for the low grog shops, kept secretly by foreigners, the committals to the watch-house, would not amount to one in a month, and this difficulty we hope to remedy within the year. The watch-house is now used to keep seized liquors instead of drunkards—and through the waste ways of the lock-up, condemned liquors are passed off into the common sewers, without having fulfilled their mission of ruin and death to our citizens. * * *

NEAL DOW, MAYOR.

FROM PROF. MOSES STUART, OF ANDOVER.

People of Maine! The God of Heaven bless you for acheiving such a victory. Many triumphs have been acheived in the good cause, but none like yours. Others have more or less fought with the drunkards and the liquor sellers, in the way of arguments and moral suasion, and indirect and inefficient and temporizing legislation. You have followed the most adroit conqueror the world has ever seen, in your scheme of policy or struggle. You have steered for the capital itself, with all its magazines and materials of war; and these once in your hands, you know the contest cannot long continue. Whence are the arms and ammunition and rations to come, when all their deposits are seized? You have the unspeakable advantage of *making war upon all the supplies of war*, and not directly upon the *men* who take the field against you. You combat with the body of sin and death itself, and not with those who are deceived and misled. You do not purpose to destroy those who are misled and drawn to ruin, but to cripple and annihilate the power that misleads them. It is an elevated and noble purpose. When mighty conquerors and crafty politicians will be forgotten, the laurel on your brows will be freshening and blooming with a beauty and glory that will be immortal.

* * * * * *

I know well what liquor dealers and distillers will say. They allege that their property is taken away, and their means of living prohibited. Very well, but what is your property? It has been applied to procure means to corrupt and destroy the community. Counterfeiters lay out large sums to procure dies for stamping coins, and plates for imitating the best bank bills. Are their establishments to be protected? The erectors of those dreadful places (rightly called) *Hells*, expend very large sums, and adorn them with magnificence. Must the community respect this property? Even honest men erect a slaughter-house, or a manufactory with noisome gases issuing from it, in the midst of a city or town. Is this property to be protected? Men adulterate medicines, and congress rises up to a man and forbids it, not only by legislation but by active inspecting officers. Are they not in the right? But—are they consistent? There are hundreds of thousands of hogsheads of adulterated liquor, much of it containing rank poison, over which they exercise no inspection and submit it to no examination. Is this a due protection of the ignorant and unsuspecting part of community? Scores of thourands die every year through the influence of these poisons. * * * And have society no remedy against all this? Maine has nobly said THEY HAVE. She has spoken with trumpet-tongue, that which eternal truth will sanction. Talk of *property* in the means of corrupting, and destroying the community! Why, then the robber's cave, and the counterfeiter's shop, where his expensive work is done, is property to be respected. Even the innocent and industrious man, if he undertakes a business which poisons the air and endangers the life of the citizens, is at once compelled to relinquish his station. How can any man rightly own that as property which sends forth pestilence and death through a whole community?—The plea for property is idle. It is unworthy a moment's regard.

So long as Legislatures pursued the criminal *personally*, so long they were sure to be met with false testimony to screen them, and abundance of sympathy with them because of their penalties. It took them longer than one would imagine to find out and beleive that drunkards and the makers of drunkards will lie. The discovery is made at last.—Maine has now lain its hand on that which can tell no lies, and that with which no honest man can sympathize.

Yes; destroy it as you would a poisonous well, or a hyena, or a tiger, without remorse and without mercy. Stand between the living and the dead, and stay the plague. Say—Thus far hast thou come, with wasting and desolation in thy train, but not a step farther shalt thou advance. Nor isthis all. *Retreat* forthwith. Abandon the ground, thou foul fiend, which thou hast occupied; yea make a speedy and a final retreat. We will bear thy presence no longer, and if thou delayest, we will sweep thee away with the besom of destruction.

The letter from which the following extract is taken, was addressed to the Hon. NEAL DOW, of Portland, Me., for the purpose of securing from him, as the framer of the Maine Liquor Law, answers direct to the questions herein proposed. A part only of the letter is given—sufficient to show the object for which it was written:—

HOMER, Cortland Co., N. Y., Nov. 10, 1852.

DEAR SIR:— * * * * *

* * It is proper for me to state in this connection, that I desire your answer to this for publication and distribution, with other Maine Liquor Law documents.

Your Law is assuredly to become the Law of the land, and its honorable author will be held in grateful and everlasting remembrance by the millions, who are to participate in its benefits, and live under its benign influence.

Permit me, then, dear sir, to propose a few questions, which may form the subject of your reply to this note, and which, may I not hope you will find time to answer, amid the thousand calls, which press upon you from every quarter of our land:—

Question 1st—Is the Law generally sustained in the towns, villages and cities of your State?

Question 2d—Is it a popular Law with your people and Legislature?

[By *popular*, I mean a favorite Law, or one readily and cheerfully sustained. Under this question, please state some general facts, and the result of your Election in September.]

Question 3d—What is the influence of the Law on business generally? As first, does it increase or diminish the value of real estate? Second, does it aid or retard the collection of debts?—the fulfilling of contracts? &c., &c. Third, are your leading business men, some of whom at first opposed the Law, now generally in favor of it, or against it?

Question 4th—What is the moral influence of the Law over your State? First, as seen in its effects upon the social circle? Second, its effects throughout the community in the decreese of vice, and crime, and poverty, and taxes, and criminal prosecutions, and general immorality among the people?

Any other intelligence bearing on this subject you may please communicate, will be most thankfully received, and will be put to the best possible use; and as I am anxious to publish these papers for distribution immediately, a reply at your earliest convenience will greatly oblige

Your friend and fellow laborer in the cause of Humanity,
ORLANDO LUND.

Hon. Neal Dow, Portland, Maine.

Portland, Me., Nov. 23, 1852.

Dear Sir:—Your favor of the 10th arrived during my absence from home, and I avail myself of the first opportunity after my return to answer your inquiries, as to the workings of the Maine Law in Maine.

The Law is generally sustained throughout the State, particularly in the larger towns and cities, where the most difficulty in its execution might have been expected.

It has already wrought a great change in the condition of the State—there being vastly less intemperance, poverty and crime than there were before. It is safe to say, that the amount of liquors sold in this State, is not more than one-tenth as great as before the Law.

The Maine Law is extremely popular in this State. The interest felt in it is such, that our last State Election turned entirely on that question, and the result was more than three to one of the Representatives in its favor, and only four Senators out of thirty-one, opposed to it. On its passage, it had of the Representatives, 86 to 40; of the

Senators, 18 to 10. The new Legislature is much stronger for the Law than that. The last Election has completely annihilated all opposition to the Law, and it will stand *as the fixed policy of the State.*

The effect of the Law upon business must be in the highest degree salutary—stimulating every branch of honest industry. The vast amount of money heretofore spent for spirits—at least $4,000,000 annually in this State—will now be spent for food, raiment, shelter, school books and all other articles of merchandise and manufacture, needful to a comfortable subsistence. All the money hitherto squandered in the grog-shops, will now be expended among all branches of legitimate trade, with a large amount in addition, which will be earned by reformed men, by their improved habits of industry. No branch of trade but the rum trade will suffer by the Maine Law.

This effect of the Law is now so obvious, that influential business men give it their hearty support, whereas, at first, they stood aloof from it.

The *moral* influence of the Law is very great—many men, formerly very intemperate, being now reformed, and extreme poverty almost unknown—in many towns the rum traffic being entirely unknown, and intemperance has consequently disappeared, while habits of industry have been greatly improved.

The returns from our Alms Houses, Houses of Correction, Jails and Watch Houses, show a striking diminution of poverty, vice and crime, although the Law is only eighteen months old while the records of our Criminal Courts show a corresponding result.

Peace and good order now reign, where riot and disorder formerly prevailed. Similar results have been uniformly obtained in Massachusetts and Rhode Island, whenever the Law has been enforced.

I agree with you entirely in the opinion, that this Law, or a similar one, will be adopted throughout the country, as the benefits resulting from it are so many and great, while no ill consequences flow from it.

It is only necessary to call the attention of intelligent men to the enormous evils of the rum traffic, to obtain their co-operation in the great work of its extinction.

I forward to you a few tracts, containing details of the workings of the Law in this city. Respectfully yours,

NEAL DOW.

ORLANDO LUND, Esq., Homer, Cortland Co., N. Y.

CONSTITUTIONAL QUESTION.

For more than two centuries, the traffic in intoxicating liquors has been licensed and regulated by law; and under the ordinances for trade, the Constitution of the United States has made certain provisions for the reception and disposition of brandies, &c., received from foreign countries. In the general burst of indignation against the traffic, called by a distinguished jurist, "a traffic in the souls and bodies of men," laws have been passed, which, in their operations, would bar these articles from sale. A question has hence arisen, Is not such entire prohibition in conflict with the laws of the General Government? The question first came up in a legal form in the State of Massachusetts, in 1837, in an exception to the the conviction of Benjamin Kimball for selling spirituous liquors without license, which conviction was considered null and void, on the ground that a law, prohibiting the sale of liquors without license, was at variance with the laws and Constitution of the United States. The Supreme Judicial Court, in this case, denied that all license and prohibitory statutes fall within the powers necessary to the police, internal regulation, and welfare of the community, and do not in the least interfere with the Constitution of the United States. A very able argument was made on this point by Hon. Peleg Sprague. The question came up again in 1845, in an appeal of Samuel Thurlow from a decision of the Courts of Massachusetts to the Supreme Court of the United States. The case was argued before that high tribunal by Messrs. Webster, Choate and Hallett, for the plaintiff; and Ashel Huntington, of Salem, for the State. Mr Webster argued that Congress alone has the power to regulate commerce with foreign nations, and among the several States, and with the Indian tribes; and that, while the law of Congress authorises importation for the sale for consumption, the law of the State prohibits all sale and consumption, and thus render invalid the law of the nation "The right," said he, "implies the right to sell, to the unrestricted use of all the channels of commerce, even to the most minute to the consumer." In opposition to Mr. Webster, Mr. Davis for the State, argued that police laws "may be carried to any extent the public welfare demands. If the health, the morals, and the welfare of the public demand the exclusion of an evil, there is a right to shut it out, regardless of revenue and private interest. If excessive indulgence in the use of intoxicating drinks be an evil, it is the right of the Legislature to guard against it by wise and prudent legislation. This restraint upon the sale of spirits, only follows out a principle maintained and enforced in all ages by civilized nations."

Mr. Webster in reply, "agreed that the retail trade should be regulated; that the State was the sole and uncontrolled judge of her policy; and that he claimed for the Court no power to review her decision on that point. He only claimed that State laws must yield when they come in conflict with the acts of Congress." The Court unanimously decided that the law of Massachusetts, forbidding the sale in less quantities than twenty-eight gallons, and the law of New Hampshire forbidding the sale in any quantity, "were not inconsistent with the Constitution of the United States, nor with any acts of Congress." And they fully established the right of a State to prohibit entirely the sale of intoxicating drinks.

Chief Justice Taney :—"Every State may regulate its own internal traffic, according to its own judgment, and upon its own views of the interest and well being of its citizens. I am not aware that these principles have ever been questioned. If any State deems the retail and internal traffic in ardent spirits injurious to its citizens, and calculated to produce idleness vice, or debauchery, I see nothing in the Constitution of the United States to prevent it from regulating and restraining the traffic or from prohibiting it altogether, if it thinks proper. The law of New Hampshire is a valid law; for although the gin sold was an import from another State, and Congress have already the power to regulate such importations, yet as Congress has made no regulation on the subject, the traffic in the article may be lawfully regulated by the State, as soon as it is landed in its territory, and a tax imposed upon it or a license required, or the sale altogether prohibited, according to the policy which the State may suppose to be its interest or its duty to pursue." All the Associate Justices agreed with the Chief Justice in this result.

Mr. Justice McLean :—"The acknowledged police power of a State extends often to the destruction of property. A nuisance may be abated. It is the settled construction of every regulation of commerce, that no person can introduce into a community malignant diseases. or anything that contaminates its morals, or endangers its safety. Individuals in the enjoyment of their own rights must be careful not to injure the rights of others."

Mr. Justice Catron :—"I admit as inevitable that, if the State has the power of restraint by licenses to any extent, she has the discretionary power to judge of its limit, and may go to the length of prohibiting sales altogether, if such be her policy; and that if this court cannot interfere in the case before us, neither could we interfere in the extreme case o exclusion.'

Mr. Justice Daniel entirely concurred in the decision of the court, but protested against the doctrine that the State cannot control the sale of an imported article by the importer, or in the original bulk or quantity.

Mr. Justice Woodbury :—"There is no contract, express or implied in any act of Congress, that the owners of property, whether importers or purchasers from them, shall sell their articles in such quantities, or at such times as they please, within the respective States. Nor can they expect to sell on any other, or better terms than are allowed by each State to all its citizens. I go further on this point than some of the court, and wish to meet the case in front, and in its worst bearings. If these laws were in the nature of partial or entire prohibition; to sell certain articles within the limits of a State, as being dangerous to public health or morals, it does not seem to me that their conflict with the Constitution would be clear. Whether such laws could be classed as police measures, or regulations of their internal commerce, is of little consequence, if they are laws, which, from their nature and object must belong to all sovereign States. Call them by whatever name, if they are necessary to the well being and independence of all communities they belong to the reserved rights of States. The States stand properly on their own powers and sovereignity, to judge of the expediency and wisdom of their own laws."

Mr. Justice Grier:—"It is not necessary to array the appalling statistics of misery, pauperism and crime, which have their origin in the use or abuse of ardent spirits. The police power, which is exclusively in the States, is alone competent to the correction of these great evils, and all measures of restraint or prohibition necessary to effect the purpose are within the scope of that authority. If a loss of revenue should accrue to the Untted States, from a diminished consumption of ardent spirits, she will be the gainer a thousand fold in the health, wealth, and happiness of the people."

This decision gave universal joy to the friends of Temperance throughout the country.

Said the Boston Standard:—

"We receive this information with tears of joy, and send it forth on the wings of the wind with a glad and exultant heart. It awakens in our heart emotions of profound gratitude to the God of Justice, that, in his good providence, we have been permitted to live to hear these glad tidings of great joy. It stirs the blood, the deepest fountains of sympathy within us, as we think of the blessings that will follow in its train; the multitudes of men who will be saved from the drunkard's grave, the wives and the children of the poor inebriate, whose tears wiped away, because the husband and father can no longer find a grog shop at every corner, and a heartless rumseller in every tavern. It inspires us with strength to labor, with faith to sustain and impel us yet higher, and nobler more comple e triumph."

Said the Rhode Island Pledge:—

"This decision will be hailed by the friends of Temperance and of good order, with the liveliest feelings of joy and pride; for it forms an epoch in the history of the Temperance reform, which, if we mistake not, will be the harbinger of a still brighter aspect of things, and to which many an important event will be referred, which is now in the uncertain future."

Said the New Haven Fountain:—

"This anxiously looked for decision has at length been made known. Now all doubt as the '*Conitstutionality* of the License Law,' is swept away—all doubt, at least, which can legally affect the question,—and the pretended 'rights of the rumseller'—the *fear* of legislators relative to the power in their hands—the uncertainty of prosecuting officers, whether they have a right to discharge the duties of their office—are all, removed."

Said the New York Reformer:—

"We regard this decision as a most signal triumph of Temperance and Temperance principles."

Said the enthusiastic Worcester Cataract:—

"*The Long Agony Ended!—Sobriety and Massachusetts Law Triumphant!*—Bring out the BIG GOBLET, and filling it to the brim with pure, crystal, salubrious water from the teetotal fount—let us all drink, long life, wealth and honor to the Judges of the Supreme Bench."

PROHIBITORY UNITED STATES LAW.

The following from the Laws of the United States, passed in the year 1834, shows that the principles of the Maine Law, is no new thing, and that Congress declares it Constitutional to search for, seize and destroy intoxicating drinks under certain circumstances. All that we now ask is, that the mantle which has so kindly been placed over the poor Indian by our Government, may be extended over all who are liable to suffer from the same cause:—

LAWS OF THE UNITED STATES FOR 1834—VOL. 9, P. 133.

SECTION 20. And be it further enacted, that if any person shall sell, exchange, or give away, barter, or dispose of any spirituous liquors or wine to an Indian in the Indian country, such person shall forfeit and pay the sum of $500. And if any person shall introduce, or cause to be introduced, or attempt to introduce, any spirituous liquors or wine into the Indian country, except such supplies as shall be necessary for the United States troops, such person shall pay a sum not exceeding $300.

SEC. 22. If any Superintendent of Indian Affairs, Indian Agent, or Sub Agent, or Commandant of a Military Post, has reason to suspect, or is informed, that any white person, or Indian is about to introduce, or has introduced, spirituous liquors, or wine into the Indian country, in violation of the provisions of this section, it shall be lawful for such Superintendent, Indian Agent, or Sub Agent, or Military Officer, to cause the boats, stores, packages and places of deposit of such persons to be searched.

And if any such spirituous liquors or wine be found, the goods, boats, packages or peltries of such persons shall be seized and delivered to the proper officer, and shall be proceeded against by libel in the proper Court, and forfeited, one-half to the use of the informer, and the other half to the use of the United States.

And it shall, moreover, be lawful for any person in the United States service, or for any Indian, or white person, to take and destroy any such liquors or wine they may find in the Indian Territory, not used as supplies for the army.

SEC. 23 Treats of distilling in the Indian Territory, and makes it such a violation as to incur the fine of $1,000, and any person may inform the Commandant of any military post, whose duty it shall be to order out his troops to destroy all such property, even to the utter destruction of all buildings aud implements used in such work of distilling.

Twenty-Three Objections to the Maine Law, Considered and Answered.

I.

It is unconstitutional.

It has been decided otherwise in the Supreme Conrt of the United States. Says Chief Justsce Taney: "Every State may regulate its own internal traffic, according to its own judgment, and upon its own views of the interest and well-being of its citizens." And, says the Governor of Maine: "If we can legislate for the extermination of ravenous beasts, we may for the extermination of the greatest of evils which reduces the human form divine to a condition worse than that of savages."

II.

It destroys private property, and without compensation.

It destroys nothing legally held; nothing, which a man keeps for his own use or for lawful sale; nothing but what is confiscated by known and willful defiance of law. And who ever heard of compensation for confiscated property—for a mad dog for instance?

III.

It is a sumptuary law, interfering with a man's household.

It does so in no sense. A man may eat, and wear what he pleases; have wine, brandy and cider daily on his table; put the bottle to his neighbor's lips and make him drunken, and the Maine Law makes no interference.

IV.

It interferes with and destroys a vast amount of regular business.

So did the Gospel with the business of silver shrine making at Ephesus; so does machinery with handiwork; so do canals and railroads with turnpikes; and steam with ship navigation. What then?

V.

It renders that unlawful which has ever been held legal.

So did the law against the slave trade, and so do laws against lotteries, and gambling, and horse-racing, and others laws too numerous to mention. And why should they not? The good of community requires it.

VI.

It will prove destructive to vast liquor manufactories.

If it does, it may be a blessed thing for the community; but if we may credit their owners, these will have full employ in supplying medicine, the arts, and the Sacrament.

VII.

It will be an unwarranted and impolitic interference with the agricultural and commercial prosperity of the State.

If it renders some crops useless, it will leave the ground for others If it prevents a vast expenditure of money for one article and that worthless, it leaves it in the hands of the people for expenditure for other articles. If the ten million of dollars now expendeds for liquor, were to be expended for bread, and meat, and clothing, and furniture, and comfortable houses and education, the public would be no losers but gainers. Every branch of industry would be benefitted and millions of capital would be added to the State.

VIII.

The public are not prepared for it.

Some portions of the public are most thoroughly prepared; some fathers and mothers, some tradesmen and mechanics, some farmers and ship-owners, some drunkards and hard drinkers. The crime, the pauperism, the taxation, the suffering of the State call for it. Some men are not ready; but cannot tell the reason why; and some, because of the cravings of appetite and the love of gain, who never will be.

IX.

It can never be enforced.

This is begging the question. It was so said in Maine, but has proved otherwise. No law was ever enforced so easily. It well nigh enforces itself. It but asks for a trial.

X.

It will produce a reaction, like the Sabbath Mail Law, destructive to the cause of temperance.

It has not done it in Maine. It may not do it elsewhere; we are willing to trust it.

XI.

It goes too far, and excludes the temperate as well as the intemperate from the purchase and use of intoxicating drinks.

It goes none too far for the good of the community. If it restrains the temperate, it may prove for their own benefit, and the benefit of their children, as well as the salvation of the drunken. Philanthropy, patriotism, and religion call for it.

XII.

It prevents free trade.

So do all license laws. No man has a right to sell without license; and if the State may forbid ninety-nine in a hundred from selling, because the good of community requires it, on the same principle it may the whole.

XIII.

It disfranchises the freemen of the State; deprives them of their rights.

Rights to prey upon their fellow men; take their money and give them no equivalent; fill up poor houses, and compel the people to support them. Liquor sellers' rights!

XIV.

It will drive our trade to other States.

What if other States should adopt the Maine Law—what then? Would it not bring the trade for rum here? Surely, the liquor sellers would vote for that.

XV.

We have law enough now.

Yes, full enough to protect liquor sellers in their business, but none to protect the people from their poisons.

XVI.

It will fill the land with blood.

Not half as much as rum has. Sixteen murders have been committed in a year, in the city of New York, through rum. Two or three lives could be afforded in this conflict.

XVII.

It is sheer fanaticism.

So is every law which breaks up counterfeiting, piracy, forgery, and which would abolish war and despotism in the earth.

XVIII.

The strigency of the law would excite sympathy for the liquor sellers and greatly increase intemperance.

The experiment has been made—the vender finds no sympathy. The war is made not upon him, but upon his liquor, as vile and worthless. The drunkards forsake his shop, for he has no liquor wherewith to treat. And left alone, he quits the business as the business has quit him, and then he finds sympathy in the rest of the community.

XIX.

Moral suasion is greatly preferable.

Moral suasion is good in its place; peculiarly applicable to the poor inebriate; applicable to the honest liquor dealer, but of no more efficacy in destroying the rum trade, than it would be in destroying counterfeiting and gambling.

XX.

It is mingling temperance and politics.

How, more than all excise laws, it is difficult to tell. It is but a new way of legislating to prevent intemperance. If it interferes with the political elevation of some of its opponents, it is not the fault of the law. If it secures that election, they may not seriously object. Rum and politics have long had the ascendency, and how can any reasonably complain, even if there should be a union on the other side, if it is for the good of the people.

XXI.

The removal of the traffic from the community would be the breaking up of one of the greatest sources of human health, comfort, and social enjoyment.

Who hath wo? who hath sorrow? who hath wounds? who hath

babblings without cause?—the teetotallers, or the men blessed with the traffic? Let jails, and poor-houses, and drunken, brawling familie answer.

XXII.

It will stop off and reform all our drunkards and hard drinkers; break up the Shades; keep our young men from their smashes and sherry cobblers; stop wife whipping and murder; make Sunday a sober day, and bring on, before the people are half ready for them, the days of Millennium.

The objection is perfectly unanswerable. Even so, Amen.

Economy of the Maine Law.

What has this Law done or what is it likely to accomplish. that it should be overthrown?

In a Tract of four pages, but a brief answer can be given to these inquiries; but all right thinking people feel a deep interest in the subject.

The Maine Law was framed and enacted, to effect a radical cure of intemperance, which all admit to be the greatest evil in the land; and though but one year old, it has been adopted in Massachusetts, Rhode Island, Minnesota, Texas and the province of New Brunswick—and has passed through one branch of the Legislatures of New Hampshire, New York and Pennsylvania; and throughout almost all the States of the Union, its enactment therein is the prominent question now before the people. Why should it not stand in Maine as the fixed law and policy of the State? Who can answer?

Before the enactment of the Maine Law, there were expended by the people of this State, annually, for strong drinks, at the lowest estimate, more than TWO MILLIONS of dollars—and this expenditure involved a loss to the people in time, diminished industry, unthrifty habits and other sources of loss, to an amount of at least two millions more; so that we had an expenditure for these drinks, directly and indirectly, of at least FOUR MILLIONS of dollars per year.

Now what is the result to the State of this great expenditure for strong drinks? Have the people been the happier for it; better fed, better clad, better sheltered, better educated? No, but just the contrary. This enormous amount of four millions of dollars has been a dead loss to the people year by year; and even worse than that, for they have not only had no valuable equivalent for it, but have received that which undermines their morals and tends directly to their impoverishment and degradation; while no persons are benefitted by the rum traffic, except a few men who have grown rich in furnishing the means of ruin to their countrymen.

What a vast amount of good may be accomplished by four millions of dollars properly expended! That sum would construct a Railroad every year, as costly as the Atlantic and St. Lawrence; would furnish every city and town in the State with churches, academies, school houses, and libraries, and support comfortably all the pastors and teachers necessary for them; would construct elegant hospitals for the gratuitous accommodation of all our sick; asylums for the reception of the superannuated poor, and all the orphans in the State who have none to care properly for them; and would endow all these institutions with ample funds; would create a fund, whereby all our State and municipal taxes might be paid, so that the people of Maine would be entirely exempt from taxes for the support of government. In one word, the entire suppression of the traffic in intoxicating drinks within our borders, would render the people of Maine in a few years, in proportion to their numbers, the richest people in the world; they would be the most virtuous and the happiest people; better fed, clad, sheltered and educated, and more industrious and prosperous than any other people. Intemperance would be entirely unknown among them, except as yellow fever is known to us by a few imported cases: our jails and prisons would be tenantless, or nearly so; of paupers we should have none; or if any, so few that alms houses would not be necessary, and vice and crime would be so far reduced in amount, as to be scarcely known to exist among us.

Such will be the effect of the Maine Law, if it remain upon our statute books and be steadily enforced.

Men of Maine, is all this desirable or not? Do you prefer that rum-selling with its long train of fearful evils shall exist among us, or that it shall be suppressed, that we may enjoy the wonderful benefits of the change? For many generations, all the governments of Europe and America have felt the rum traffic to be a great evil, and have endeavored to protect their people from its effects as far as possible. All these governments have often enacted laws to regulate and restrain this traffic—they did not think it could be destroyed; but Maine has undertaken to expel this traffic entirely from her borders, and with wonderful success.

The civilized world is now looking with admiration upon this great experiment; if it succeed, the people of Maine will be happy and prosperous, and all the nations of the earth will follow her example; if it do not succeed, it will be through the indifference or timidity of professedly good men, who fear to resist bad men in their efforts to overthrow this law, which restrains their appetites and passions and affects their interests.

In the year during which this law has been in existence, its effects have been more decisive and salutary than its warmest friends had anticipated. The wholesale traffic in strong drinks has been entirely annihilated throughout the State; the grog shops are very few, and are kept in dark and secret places, so that temptation is entirely removed from the way of the young and inexperienced. The quantity of spirits now sold in the State, cannot be more than one-tenth part so great as it was before the enactment of the Maine Law, so that the saving to the people, is already at least one million eight hundred thousand dollars per year. The result of this can be seen in the improved habits and cirtumstances of our people. Many men, formerly miserable drunkards, are now perfectly sober, because temptation is removed out of their way;—many families before miserable and dependent upon the public, or upon charity for support, are now comfortably fed, clad and lodged. Our Alms Houses are not crowded as they were; their inmates are greatly diminished in number, and some of them are nearly empty. Our jails are almost tenantless, some of them entirely so; our Houses of Correction are now almost without occupants, and all this because few men become paupers or commit crimes except under the influence of strong drinks.

Why should this law be repealed? What evil has it done?

Neal Dow, Mayor of Portland, in his annual report says:—"At the commencement of the year, the number of open rum shops in full operation in the city, was supposed to be from 300 to 400; 300 was the lowest estimate; *at present there is not one.* The receipts of these places per day, at the lowest figure, may be reckoned to average three dollars; this for 300 days including Sundays—and Sundays were the best days for these places—would give $270,000 per year!

It may be thought that this sum is much too large to have been expended annually by the people of this city for intoxicating drinks, but it believed that the number of grog shops set down at 300, and the sum received by each per day, at $3, is within the fact. But if we consider the expenditure in this way to have been only $200,000, or about $2,22 per day for each of the 300 shops, the fact will be sufficiently important to arrest the attention of every man who has any regard for the prosperity of the city and the welfare of the citizens.

The whole of this sum or of whatever sum may have been expended in this way, was entirely lost to the city; no valuable return was obtained from it. This amount will purchase 40,000 barrels of flour at $5 each, or *about five barrels of flour and five cords of wood to every family in the city*, estimating the number of families at 4000. It is true some persons accumulated wealth by this traffic, but it was not by paying a fair equivalent, or any equivalent for property so gained; but the process was simply the transfering the hard earnings of the laboring man to the coffers of the dealers in spirits—while the victims of their trade were sent to theis desolate homes to abuse wives and children who were suffering for the common necessaries of life, which might have been purchased with the money squandered on strong drinks.

☞ A great many families in this city situated thus a year since, are now comfortable and happy, being entirely relieved by the suppression of the grog shops, from their former troubles. The extinguishment of the traffic in intoxicating drinks will not only be the means of saving this great amount of money to the poorer part of the people, but the productive industry of the country will be stimulated to an extent that we cannot at present foresee. The whole of the great sum which was formerly expended for strong drinks by the people of this city and State; will henceforth be expended for the necessaries and comforts of life with the additional amount which will accrue from the more industrious habits of the people, or will be added yaer by year to the accumulating wealth of the State."

Prohibitory Laws.

The terms prohibitory or sumptuary, when attached to laws, have been urged as constituting a valid objection to their enactment. This objection is intended by a certain class of citizens, to apply especially to laws restraining the traffic in intoxicating liquors, as a violent restraint on civil liberty.

No matter what names you give such laws; while they are required by the public good they afford no reasonable ground of complaint, as a restraint on civil liberty. Has the distiller in years gone by, been forbidden under a penalty of $300 to use leaden pipes? Does the State of Maine, under a penalty of $1,000 and imprisonment, prohibit the sale in the shambles of the ox that died of disease? May not our Board of Health prohibit both the sale and purchase of fish, fruit and vegetables, as long as public health may requirr it? And who withhold obedience to such ordinances, because they are sumptuary, dietetic or prohibitory? Should an article be sold in our shops or administered, like that Eugene Sue has described as used in France for securing death by a slow poison, would it not be an offence cognizable by law? And how else could it be kept out of society and shops, than by prohibitory enactments? Even after brurjed away from the sight of friends such laws keep watch by our tomb. Nor will any dare, but under severe forfeiture, to disturb the inanimate body, or mar, with ruthless finger, our marble slab. Such an office do prohibitory laws discharge: If we examine the digest of our own State, we shall there find, line upon line, and precept upon precept, of a prohibitory character,

It would be a libel on society, to suppose, it too imbecile, to thus have the means of self preservation. The constitution of society is based on foundations deep and broad enough to resist the storms of human passions. Prohibitory restraints are our protection; whoever would avoid them, must leave society at least, if not the the world.

Life, character and morals; commercial credit, peculiar interests and bodily health are under their protection; any discredit cast upon laws necessary for public good; any disparaging of their influence, are wounds on the body politic; for these laws are the staff of society—if we weaken this prop, we break the only support whereon we lean, and must, in turn, be pierced through with many sorrows.

Prohibitory laws regulate the style, height and material of our tenements. They even enter our stores and kitchens and prescribe what cannot be allowed in the one and the other; they descend to all the minutiæ of life; the details of trade; they show us where powder shall be kept, and how pork must be packed; where hay can be sold, and the manner scythes are to be carried; how shad and salmon may be caught, and when only moose and deer may be killed; nor can a sparrow fall to the ground without their notice. So omniscient are prohibitory laws, they

"Live through all life, extend through a.l extent,
Spread undivided, and operate unspent."

The fish of the sea, fowl of the air, and beast of the field fall within the empire of law—and if these smaller matters are heeded by it, how much more weighty subjects for its exercise, are the rational members of society.

Our very senses are protected by prohibitory laws—noxious exhalations, indecent print, obscene and blasphemous language are all prohibited; does not intemperance produce at the corners of our streets, in the concourse of the people much more cognizable offences in its tableaux vivants!

If prohibitory laws protect the very stone at our grave from ruthless fingers, how much more ought they to defend from that which destroys the image of God in the soul, blots out our conscience and throws down the monument of our immortality.

If the stupid ox, which indeed knoweth its owner is protected from inhuman treatment under a penalty of $200, how much more need of the protection of the prohibitory law has the fool, whom "though thou shouldst bray in a mortar, among wheat with a pestle, yet will not his foolishness depart from him.',

If the cognomen prohibitory or sumptuary, when attached to laws, constitutes a valid objection to their enactment then society has not the means of self presevation. Of all subjects for legislation, we conceive intemperance a fair one—and the multiform evils growing out of it, make it a crying sin—yea, as is "an iniquity to be punished by the Judges Law."

Look at Your Taxes.

One day, while walking the streets of Albany, Mr. E. C. Delavan met a friend, whom he thus accosted—

"Mr. C,, do you know there is a mortgage on your property?"

"Why, no, sir," said Mr. C,, "my property is free and unincumbered."

"But there is a mortgage upon it," said Mr. Delavan. "I have examined the records, and I find that you pay one thousand dollars taxes, and over six hundred dollars of that goes to pay for Intemperance. Your property is is mortgaged to the rumsellers of Albany for $10,000, and you have to pay the interest every year; and if you were to die to-morrow, it would go to your heirs with that incumbrance, and they would have to pay up the interest regularly, or it would be sold by the sheriff."

Here, then, was an astounding truth developed to Mr. C., and if it was truth to Mr. C., it is no less so to every property holder in the State of New York. We invite such to contemplate it. Look at it unflinchingly, ye who groan under the burdens of taxation. See for whom it is that ye gain money in the sweat of your brow: by whom, it is wrested from you; and who they are that are fattening on your toils.

That we reason not at random, we take you to the Report of the Legislative Committee on the Excise question in March 1850, From returns, says the Report made to the Secretary of State, the cost of pauperism in 1849, was 817.441. Of this, the Report estimates $670,143 for Intemperance. Were there no dram shops and no Intemperance, the whole cost of supporting the poor, would be but $147,298. Taxation for crime, says the Report, it is diffinult to estimate. One trial for murder has recently cost the county of Albacy $600. Another, the county of Orleans, $1,000. Nearly all the business of grand juries, sheriffs, constables and almost the entire police system in all the cities, is chargeable to Intemperance. People of the Empire State! have not the Liquor sellers a mortgage on your property, and do they not wrench from you, year after year, the fruit of your hard labors? But to come to cities and counties. W. Edmonds, Esq,. Warden of the Tombs in the City of New York, reported in 1849, 18,042 commitments. Of these, 4,207 males and 4,748 females were charged with the grossest and most debasing intoxication; 3,495 persons were imprisoned for acts committed in a state of intoxication, 2,249 were vagrants, each a common vagabond, sent to the Penitentiary, because unfit for the Alms House; 231 lunatics deprived of their reason by rum; 228 houseless persons cast upon public charity by the intemperance of themselves or others;—near three-fourths of those for whose support taxes were to be levied upon the property holders of the city. Look into the country. In Herkimer county, there were, in 1849, 1,739 drunken paupers, according to the report of the superintendents of poor, for whom a tax was levied of $10.950, or $565,19 to each of its nineteen towns; are caused by about 147 liquor sellers. Were they instead of the people taxed to support the drunken poor, the tax on each would have been $73,19, whereas the most they paid was $5 for license, leaving the people to pay $68,19, that they might make money, and support their families in ease. If each vender received $250 a year for his liquors, it amounted, in the aggregate, to $36,950, enough to build a school house in every town in the county, worth $1,006, hire a teacher and pay him $30 a month, and leave $607, 10 for libraries, apparatus, &c. In Ulster County, $15,000 were levied in 1845, which would not have been needed without intemperance. In Tioga County, the taxes for pauperism and crime averaged, for six years, $14,000; three-fourths were attributed to Intemperance. In fifty-four years, in Livingston County, $58,814,12 were levied upon the people for the poor and criminal justice; $44,140,60 of this according to the testimony of George Hastings, Esq., District Attorney, were for intemperance. In Orange County, the Board of Supervisors charged the county $8,047,65 for general fund; $9,000 to pay judges and jurors; poor fund, $12,000. Of this $8,000 was for Intemperance. A drunken father in that county, placed his little daughter upon an ox sled, and rudely whipping his cattle, they rushed to the road side, threw off the child and made her a cripple, and she has been supported in the poor house more than twenty years; the tax-payer and not the rumseller footing the bill. Is not your property, then, mortgaged to the liquor sellers for the support of their business? You know it is. While they are suffered to sell, drunkenness, poverty and crime of the most horrid character, will continue a burden upon the State. But we have not yet told the worst of your state. Not only is there a mortgage upon your property, but a proscription upon your sons. When Napoleon was rising to the heights of his power and trampling down the nations by his iron foot, he demanded every tenth young man when of age, for his armies; and sometimes he anticipated one, two and even three years under the plea that his interests demanded it. O what weeping and wailing was there as the young conscripts were dragged from their homes? People of the Empire State! in as merciless a tyranny and no less irresistable and certain, the rum-sellers of the State have a mark upon your sons. By examination, it has been found that one in thirty of our best population have been converted into common drunkards; that the farming districts have lost in deaths by Intemperance about 30 per cent. among the male adults; the village about fifty; that of 680 maniacs in various Asylums, 400 owed their loss of reason to intoxicating liquors; and that 400 out of 600 juvenile delinquents either drank themselves or were the children of drinking parents. Yes! rumsellers have a merciless proscription upon your children. You must not only give them your property, but your sons. They will drag them from your dwellings before the eyes of Fathers and Mothers, and throw them into loathsome dungeons and put them to early deaths. They are doing it every day and every hour. They fill up your grave yards, and Rachael refuses to be comforted because her children are not. How long will you suffer it? How long shall the terrific power rage and rend and devor? It promises you compensation for its license, But what compensation can it make for your stolen property; what for your lost sons? Why license—why permit it all? What are your school taxes—your taxes for the Gospel—your taxes for public improvement and for protection? Not to be named with rum taxes, and all cheerfully paid, because pouring into your bosom rich blessings.

And ther again your voluntary taxation;—money spent by yourselves and the people of America for intoxicating liquors. We ask you to look at that, and see how ignominiously you bend to the rumsellers' yoke.

The common school fund of the State of New York, the literature fund, the Bank fund would not pay the cost of liquor drank in the country in twenty-five days. The American Bible Society did not cost the country so much in twenty-four years of its operation, as has strong drink in seventeen days. The inhabitants of the Empire State now tax themselves voluntarily, every year twenty-six millions of dollars, in addition to what they are compelled to pay, in direct taxes for strong drinks, enough to build each year an Erie Canal and Croton Water Works. You are a father with a dependant little family around you. You find it perhaps difficult to feed and clothe them. Do you use 6¼ cents' worth of liquor a day, you voluntarily tax yourself twenty-two dollars a year for that which is to you of no essential value? The money saved, might give them more comforts than you can readily imagine, besides saving you from destruction This mortgage upon your estate you can lift in a moment, by adopting the total abstinence principle. And you can lift the other also, ye Yeoman, of the Empire State, if ye will. Your sister, Maine, has done it. She will have no rumseller in her borders. She have no taxes created by the trade, no men made paupers nor excited to crime. The two millions of dollar she has squandered upon intoxicating liquors, she has wisely resolved she will expend upon her farms and her houses, her schools, her churches for the improvement and advancement of the State. The rights of trade will, it is posssible, interpose a veto. But what are the rights of trade? Never the right to traffic in an article which spreads desolation through the community. If the people will not demand by legislation protection to themselves and their children from this enormous taxation, laid for no good object, but for one full of evil, they deserve to be hewers of wood and drawers of water to the most useless and despicable class of traders. How can they plead on the Fourth of July, a descent from men who would not pay a paltry tax on tea because it was laid without their consent? Who of you consent to the enormous rum taxes you pay? All who consent to the license system and the continuance of the traffic. Wake, then, to a sense of the burdens which are upon you Use no violence to burst the chains; but go steadily and firmly to the polls, and it will dissolve away before the indignant voice of a people resolved to be free.

Shall we have the Maine Law?

What is it?

It is a new experiment for the suppression of Intemperance. The fountains of Intemperance are the supply of intoxicating liquors, first in hospitality but chiefly for gain; as an article of trade. The first it does not touch; only the second—the sale for gain. For two hundred years this has been regulated by law, that it should not prove disastrous to the community, yet it has proved disastrous under the best regulations. The Maine Law is an experiment at remedying the evil by its entire suppression. It forbids all sale of intoxicating and spirituous liquors as a common beverage. It confiscates and consigns to destruction by the public magistrate, all such liquors kept on sale, except for medicine and the arts. And in addition the loss of liquor, it punish the offender, with fine and imprisonment to secure universal obedience. Such is the Maine Law. It does not prohibit the use, only the sale as a beverage.

What would it do for us, if we had it?

Much every way. In the first place it would greatly reduce our taxes. More than two thirds of the taxation caused by pauperism and crime, is the result of intemperance, From the official returns made to the Secretary of the State of New York, the cost of pauperism in 1849 was $8.7,441. Of this $670,143 was set down to intemperance. But intemperance flows from the traffic. The supply creates the demand. Shut up the traffic, and intemperance and its results would soon cease. The taxes now paid for the erection of poor houses and jails and the support of paupers, and the trial and punishment of criminals would be but trifling.

2. It would save a vast amount of physical suffering. Who hath woe? Who hath sorrow? Who hath contention? Who hath wounds without cause? What class of all others have privation and want, hunger, cold and nakedness, oppression and cruelty, physical and mental agony, like drunkards and drunkards' families? Give us the Maine Law, and the haggard harpey, fixing his talons deep, is fled away,

3. It would prevent a mighty flood of moral evil. The liquor business is the prolific mother of crime. The dram shop is the hot bed of iniquity. There generate and ripen to the maturity of hell, every abomination;—debate, discord, murder, blasphemy, lust, arson, Sabbath breaking, defiance of God, of death and judgment, Shut it up hroughout the State and nation, and in one half year one fifths of all that now ascends to draw the lightning's flash from the throne of God would cease for ever.

4. It would save us a vast amount of property. The vender says he gives an equivalent for all the money he receives It is false. He knows it. Did the buyer pour out his liquor upon the ground the moment he bought it, he would be as rich as if he kept and used it. It would not be so with food, and clothing, and fuel. If he destroyed them, he would be a loser to the full extent. Money spent for liquor is a waste; and what a waste! Millions of dollars in a State a dead loss every year, besides the loss of the labor of the drunken; the cost pauperism and crime; the private charities; money wasted in dissipation and foolish bargains; losses by fires and shipwrecks, more than a hundred millions annually in the nation. More than two millions of dollars are saved by the Maine Law to the State of Maine in a year, to be expended on clothing, and farms, dwellings, and roads, and to be used in business for the benefit of families and prosperity of the State. What would be saved by such a law in the State of New York, of Pennsylvania, of Ohio, of Illinois; and how soon would all the people in these States be better clad and better fed, and better sheltered, and better educated; and how much better, who can tell?

5. It would ensure great peace and quietness. The liquor shops have caused three-fourths of the brawls, fights, riot and disturbances in every city and town. Of 180,646 persons committed in six and a half years in the City of New York, 18,793 were for assault and battery, 25,164 for disorderly conduct, 3,645 for fighting in the street, 44,383 for intoxication, 35,048 for intoxication and disorderly conduct, and 14,800 for vagrancy, making 140,783 for offences resulting almost entirely from the use of liquor in dram shops. Out of these dens of vice rush men who holloa, disturb neighborhoods, cause fights and murders, and put fire to buildings and call out the watch and fill up the Tombs and Penetentiaries. Where the Maine Law has gone into operation, there is comparative peace and quietness; and a police are almost unneeded. In Portland, the commitments to the House of Correction were reduced in nine months three fourths. In Bangor, the House of Corrections has been almost empty. In Augusta, the Police had been formerly called out an hundred nights in the year; during the year of the law not once. In Providence, for weeks before the law, there were from twenty to forty commitments; in the week after, only six;—so it will be anywhere with the Maine Law, almost realising the prediction, "Violence shall no more be heard in the stands, wasting nor destruction in thy borders."

6. It would result in the reform of almost every inebriate. Deprived of the means of easy indulgence, and temptation removed, drunken men would soon, of necessity, and soon, of choice, become sober men, and be thankful for their deliverance from their most horrid thraldom.

"I never expected," said an habitual drunkard to the Mayor of Bangor," to die a sober man, but I believe I shall." "The law is popular," says the Cashier of the Bank of Calias, "with the best of inebriates, who feel themselves to be the slaves of a depraved appetite, and wish to be free." The law would at once reclaim many a drunkard, and make the State an Asylum where he could live in safety.

7. It would prevent hundreds and thousands of young men from becoming drunkards. Men might still somewhere obtain liquor, and drink and be drunken. The gay the fashionable, the men of wealth and luxury might put the bottle to their neighbors' lips, and train their offspring to be miserable inebriates, to curse and torment them in their declining years and none might hinder, but the work, the desolating work of the gay saloon, of the tavern bar, of the low groggery, would have ceased. The great manufactories in which live men are converted into wild beasts and made food for the fires of hell, would be all stopped. Their fires would be put out.

8. It would save the Sabbath from its worst desecration and deliver religion from its worst foe. No desecration of the Sabbath has ever been like that caused by the liquor trade, and no obstacle like intemperance has been known to the salvation of the soul. "When the Maine Law," says the venerable Lyman Beecher, "passes through the land: the millenium will be right on its heels. Then the devil will lose his strong hold. He will be bound neck and heels and thrown into the bottomless pit." This is what the law would do for us.

But how shall we get it?

Go to the ballot box and choose legislators who will give it. There are men enough of both and all political parties capable of doing all the business of legislation, who will give us the law. Vote for them and for none others, and it will be ours.

And now shall we have it?

Why not?

It will break up the liquor sellers business.

No matter for that. His business is a bad one, of benefit to none, and destructive to thousands.

It will waste much property.

And it will save much; millions on millions.

It will cause much contention.

Not a thousandth part as much as rum has.

It will overthrow our political party.

Does our political party stand on rum? If so, let us be ashamed of it, and quit it. But let us take heed lest our political party is soon in the minority, from its adherence to rum, for it surely will be. Degeneracy and subserviency to wickedness and debasement is not the spirit of the age. God will overturn, and overturn, and overturn until temperance and truth are triumphant.

We may ourselves want occasionally some brandy, or gin, or wine, and do not love to be deprived of the opportunity of getting them.

And so we never may want them. Hundreds and thousands of the best and most laborious families in the land have for years lived without them and never needed them, and so may we; and what if we do, shall we not gladly sacrifice our desires on the altar of public good.

Shall ye not then have the Maine Law?

Say, ye Fathers! speak for your sons.

Say, ye Mothers! speak for your daughters.

Say, young men! speak for your country.

Say, ye ministers of the Gospel! speak for thousands perishing in sin.

Say, Philanthropist! bending over fallen husbands and bleeding families.

Say, Patriot! asking for glory for your country.

Say, all. All answer; ten thousand voices answer, answer now; answ at the polls and answer all, in the halls of Legislation—Yes, Yes!

[From a Baltimore paper.]

NATIONAL LEGISLATION.

AS RELATING TO THE TEMPERANCE REFORM.

Mr. Editor.—I take up my pen in the confident expectation that the importance of the "end and aim" of this communication will furnish a sufficient apology for troubling you with it. The movement in behalf of legislation for the suppression of the traffic in intoxicating beverages, now on foot in several of the states of our confederacy, after the glorious example of Maine, is revealing a most important contradiction, if not a direct conflict, between that more thorough legislative control, so desirable in these states, and the existing policy of the General Government, touching the same interest. Thus, Maine has been compelled to make an exception in favor of the "original packages" of poisonous liquids, as they come from the custom houses; and while she has placed upon her statute book a law which, though thus circumscribed, has conferred immortal honor upon her sons, the more virtuous and orderly of whom now are sustaining it, the nation retains upon its statute book a law which sanctions the importation of these same poisonous liquids into her borders, for use as beverages, contrary to the manifest wishes of the great majority of her citizens! Should the Maine Law be enacted in this state, or others in which it is now being mooted, the same contradiction and conflict will be encountered; and thus the National Government, which ought, in all cases, to stand forth as a kind parent protecting and fostering the highest interests of the various members of the family, will be found placing barriers in the new paths wherein they may seek to walk, in search of the prosperity of themselves as individual states! According to my information, this exception, as required by the U. S. Constitution has opened the door of evasion and subterfuge to some extent, even in Portland. If so in that city, what increased difficulties may we not anticipate in such emporiums of direct foreign trade as New York? Mark well what I write. I speak not of these difficulties as insurmountable. That is the enemy's cry—not ours.

Now, apart from the foregoing considerations, there is another which should not be passed over lightly. I allude to the effect of legal sanctions upon the public sense of right and wrong—the "public conscience" of those concerned in transactions under them. Let us look at this point for a moment: There can be no doubt that the License System, as it prevails in this and other states, prompts to wrong-doing, while it shields it. Mankind have been taught to contemplate "law" with a species of reverence, and just laws are worthy of being so contemplated. But unfortunately, this reverence is too conveniently transferred to unjust laws. Thus a false measure of conscience is proffered and willingly accepted. The offender against the social good, who has found it so convenient to measure his employment by it, may be referred to the unchangeable principles of truth, and may be pointed to the glaring results of his career, but in vain. He will refer you in turn, to the State, and that theoretical embodiment of the highest idea of justice, the Statute Book, and coolly tell you that he scouts your "higher law"—that this is high enough law for him! If this be true of state laws, how much more strikingly so of national laws. There is not a man in this nation but has been taught to regard the authority, moral as well as physical, of the nation, as more commanding than that of his state; and the effect of that teaching will cling to him in more or less strength of adhesion, in spite of the unrighteousness of the nation's enactments or enforcements. It is very clear to my mind, then, that as a crowning sanction, the friends of Temperance cannot afford to forego the assistance of national law in the present struggle. The frowning battlements of national counteraction would cast shadows of gloom over the new entrenchments of state law, if suffered to exist longer, and they would dishearten the noble soldiery of Reform. What is the conclusion to which this hurried glance at things as they are, points us? Why, clearly, this: —The absolute necessity of bringing the National Government to our aid. I have been surprised to find no movement by petitions to Congress on this subject. Can it be questioned that that body has, under the Constitution, power to grant the "strong arm of the law?" It has full power over foreign commerce, and the very same class of motives which prohibited the foreign slave trade should prohibited the foreign slave trade should prohibit the foreign liquor trade also. That was, moreover, totally abolished, while we need only ask the prohibition of the importation of liquors for other than mechanical and medicinal purposes. We are not left without precedents of legislation to justify our demands upon the National Authority for aid in this direction. I may safely refer to the Embargo Act in force during the administrations of Jefferson and Madison, and which received the approbation of those great statesmen. It was a prohibitory measure of the most sweeping character; and yet the British Government, whose commerce was most effected by it, not only did not complain of it, but admitted its strict accordance with the laws of nations, as was shown by Mr. Canning's letter to Mr. Pinkney in 1808. So of the nonimportation and non-intercourse acts of the same governmental era. To which should be added, as directly applicable to the present question, that the rule of reciprocal intercourse between nations is based upon the understanding that the prosperity and happiness of the foreign country with which intercourse is sought, shall ever be regarded. This view will be found running through all the discussions of the subject in the writings of Vattel and the elder authorities generally, and also through all the later discussions. I may be told that the aforesaid acts were justified by the "necessities of the case." Grant it, and then allow the friends of Temperance the same plea in view of the woeful influence of the foreign liquor trade, as justly you must. But, fortunately for our position, we do not need to go back so far. We may successfully point to revenue laws now on the statute book, and in constant force. Among these may be cited the law against the importation of obscene books and pictures. But a few weeks ago an enforcement thereof was made in this city, whereby a large invoice of pictorial German pipes was declared contraband by the United States judicial authority, and destroyed, while a lot of otherwise lawful goods, found with them, in the "original packages," were forfeited to the Government. I might go on, and point also to the prohibition of the importation of foreign paupers, as it prevails in several of the States, without its "constitutionality" being questioned for a moment, and with that phase of the question alone I have to do at present. Now, surely, if it be constitutional to prohibit the inbringing of paupers as such—that is without the discriminative provision that they shall give security not to be at the public charge—it ought to be considered constitutional to prohibit the introduction of such pauper-making agents as those under notice. But, as I have already said, there should be no doubt on this point. The 8th section of the 1st Article of the Constitution gives Congress the authority to "regulate commerce with foreign nations, and among the several states, and with the Indian tribes." In pursuance of this authority to "regulate," laws have been passed totally prohibiting the introduction of this "fire water" among the Redmen, for use as a beverage. Why not "regulate" the general importation of foreign liquors in the same discriminating mode? Surely no one will attempt an adverse answer, when a moment's reflection will show him that, in admitting the constitutionality of such a measure of prohibition as to a portion of our territory, we are committed to its applicability to the whole, and thus the question is given up—for be it remembered the constitution claims no control, commercially, in the territories, that it does not claim, in equal measure, in the states. Other citations arise to view, but I hope I have given enough for my present purpose.

Does any truth-seeking man doubt the expediency of Congress legislating thus discrimatingly? If so, let him think of some project for importing lions and tigers, and hyenas, for other than the purposes of the menagerie—to be turned loose in the streets, for example—and ask himself what would be the course of Congress in such an emergency. To the advocates of "protection," I apprehend, the idea of a tariff so high as to prohibit the importation of foreign liquors, for even the legitimate purposes named, would not be repugnant—unless, indeed, self-interest or a perverted appetite should prompt them to shut their senses against the laws of analogy. I confess that I prefer the more direct mode of open and avowed prohibition; but I am now addressing myself to a class of readers who have no scruples on this point, and I do so with the hope of giving a temperance-promoting application of their views to the urgent social necessities of the times. Shall I appeal to them in vain?

Shall not a movement by petition to Congress begin at once. What say the friends of "legal suasion" in the States where State action has been invoked? What say the noble pioneers of Maine? Now that they have done all that can be effected by statal action, and have experienced the need of national action to back up their local movement of reform, let them see that the good work is perfected! By whom; more appropriately, could this agitation be commenced? Men of Maine! what say you to this proposal?

In closing, I think I may confidenty put this question to those into whose hands the suggestions of this letter may chance to fall. To what more sublime line of enaction could the National Legislature be directed than this?—this which gives the only reasonable hope of even the beginning of that "millennial reign" for which we find all sects of Christians praying. And is not such an anticipation hopeless, in view of the present state of things? To my mind, utterly so. If suffered to increase its seductive appliances for a few years longer, at the present rate, rum traffic would have the power to counteract the agencies of all the clergy of the earth combined! The Preacher of the Gospel in his pulpit compared with the rumseller, who will be sure to raise his altar near by, sinks in imagination, to the subordinate position of the little boy who takes his humble stand at the foot of the bowling alley, to set up the "pins," while the athletic and adroit man, who stands at the head knocks them down with "strikes" that counts by "tens!" and triumphantly wins the game.

I am aware that this is a gloomy and discouraging picture of the triumph of the spirit of evils in our land. But the truth were better told than withheld, that we may timely set ourselves to work for the securement of the remedy of thorough legal prohibition—National as well as Statal. J. E. SNODGRASS.

Baltimore, April 20, 1852.

www.ingramcontent.com/pod-product-compliance
Lightning Source LLC
LaVergne TN
LVHW011132110826
845150LV00008B/2305

* 9 7 8 1 4 1 8 1 9 4 4 0 6 *